yukismart.com/b/677e76

body

Körper

head

Kopf

face

Gesicht

grow up

heranwachsen

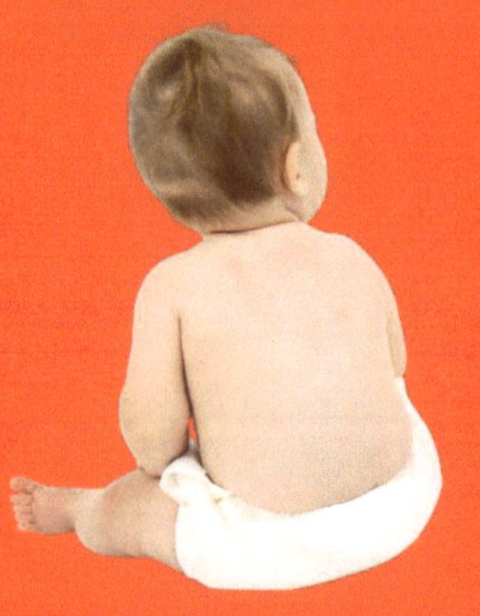

back

Rücken

chest

Brustkorb

bottom

Hintern

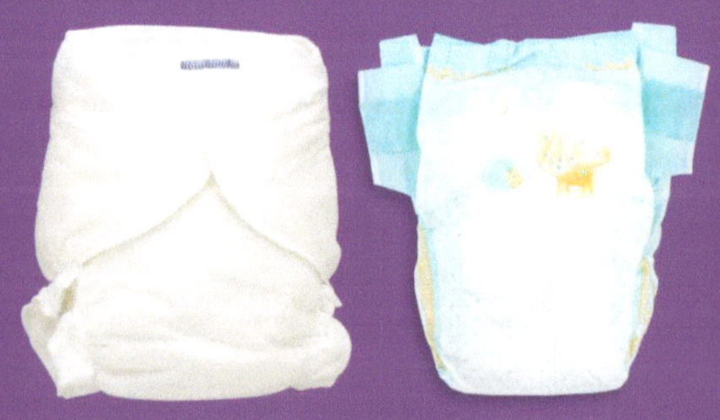

diaper

Windel

eye

Auge

glasses

Brille

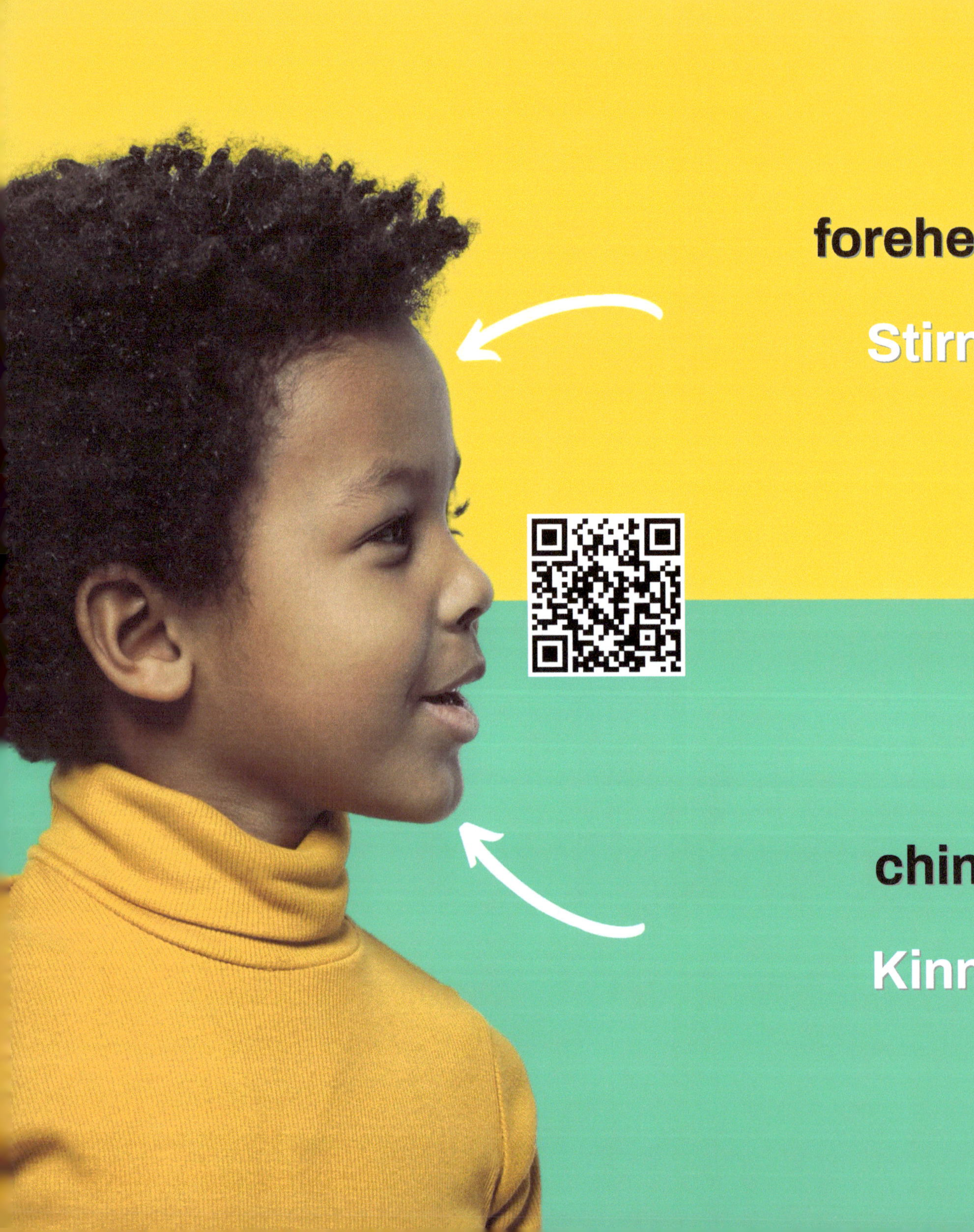

forehead
Stirn
chin
Kinn

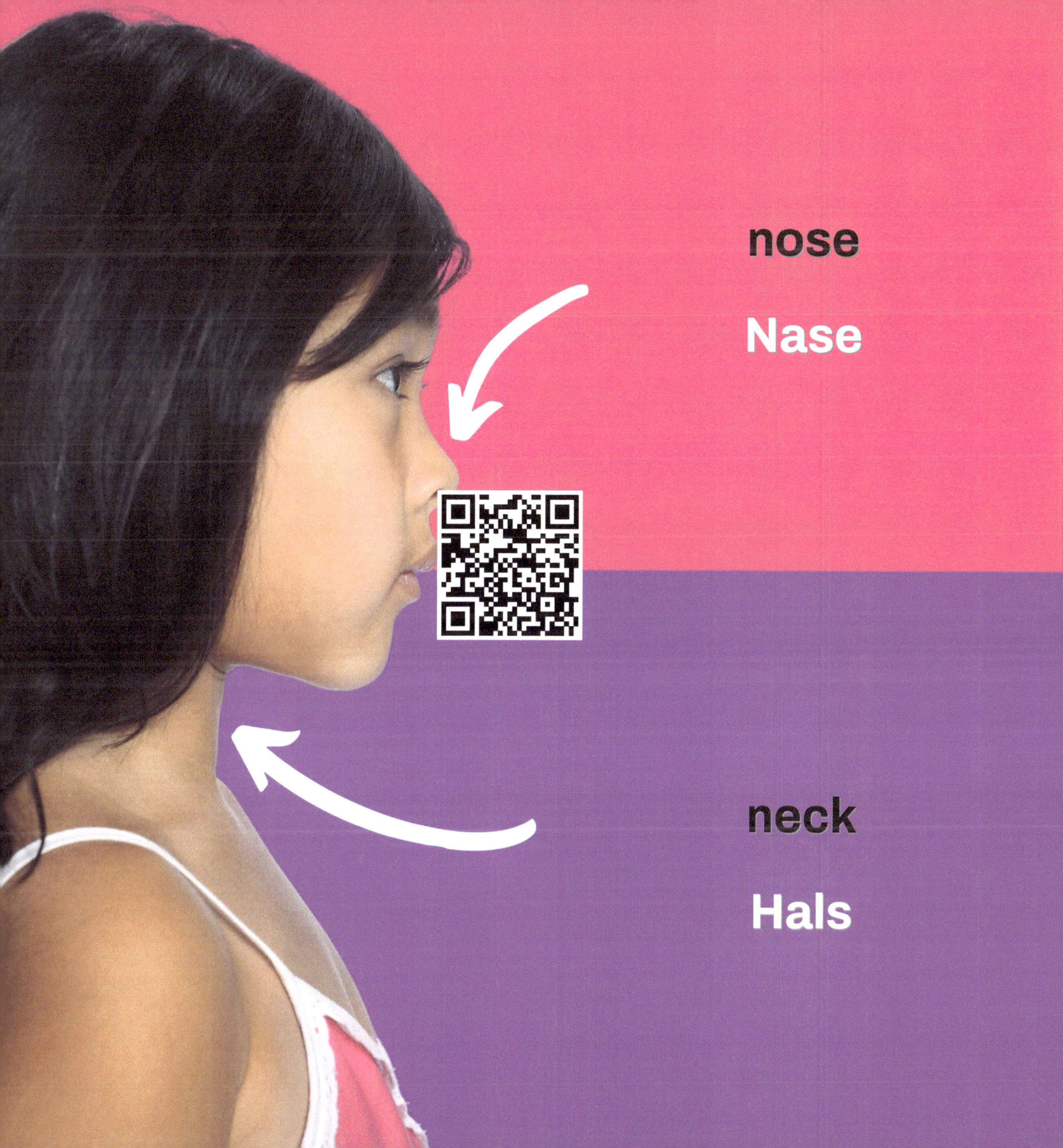

nose
Nase
neck
Hals

ear

Ohr

cheeks

Wangen

kiss

küssen

mouth

Mund

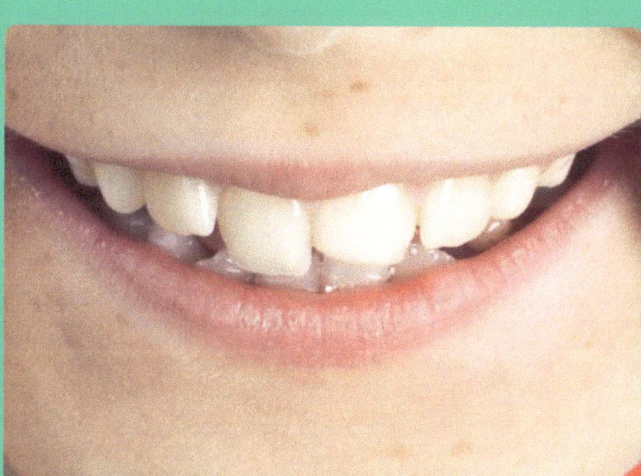

teeth

Zähne

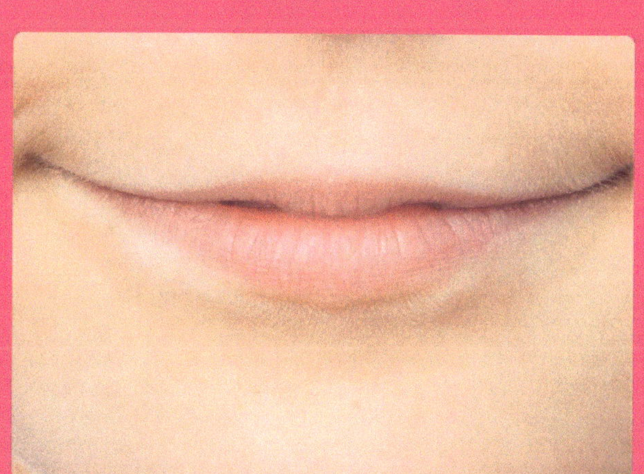

lips

Lippen

tongue

Zunge

hair

Haare

straight hair

glattes Haar

curly hair

lockiges Haar

black hair

schwarzes Haar

brown hair

braunes Haar

ginger hair

rotes Haar

blond hair

blondes Haar

gray hair
graues Haar
bald head
Glatze

beard

Bart

moustache

Schnurrbart

arm
Arm
elbow
Ellbogen

hand

Hand

fingers

Finger

thumb

Daumen

belly

Bauch

navel

Bauchnabel

foot

Fuß

leg

Bein

heel

Ferse

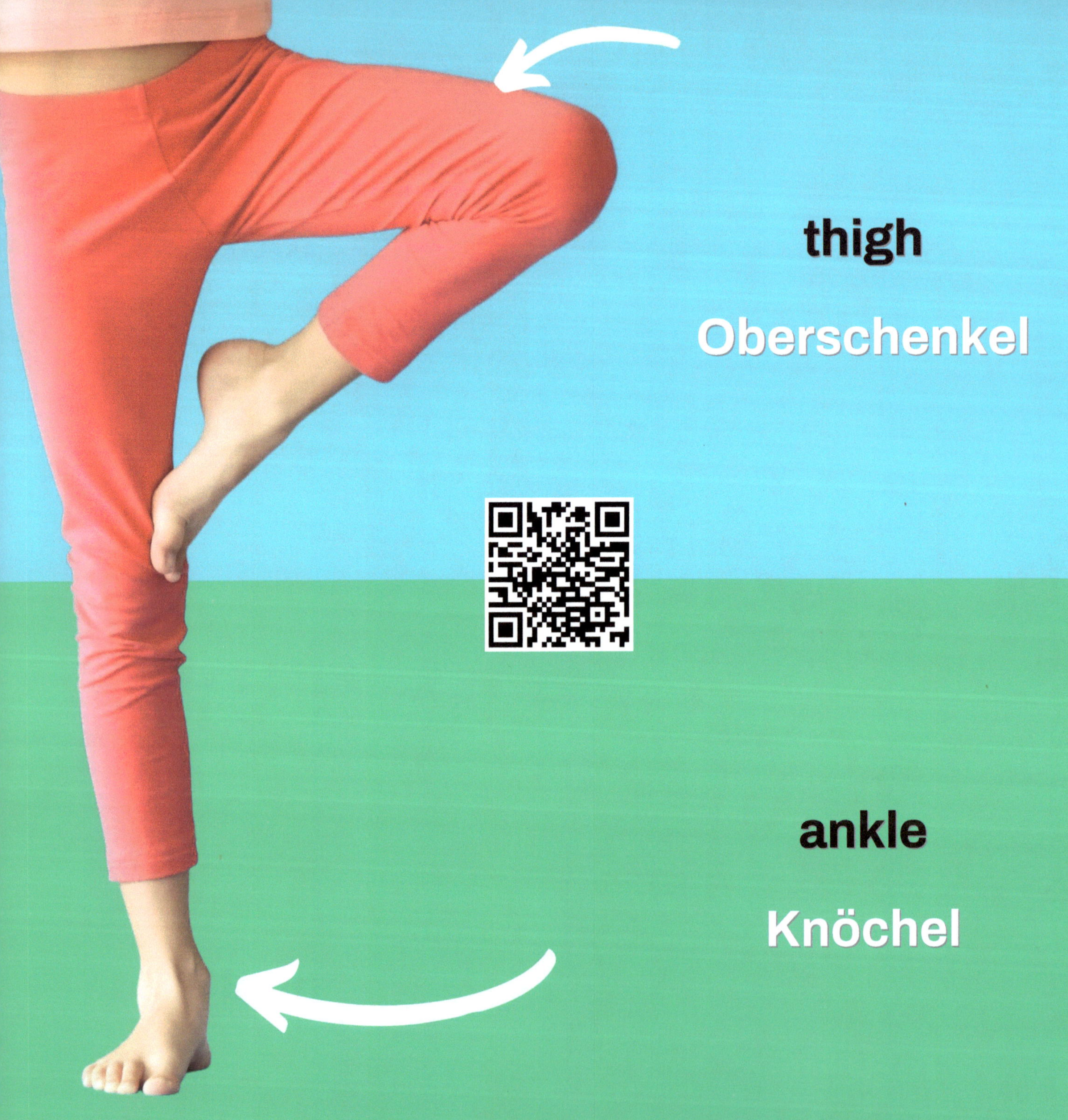

thigh
Oberschenkel
ankle
Knöchel

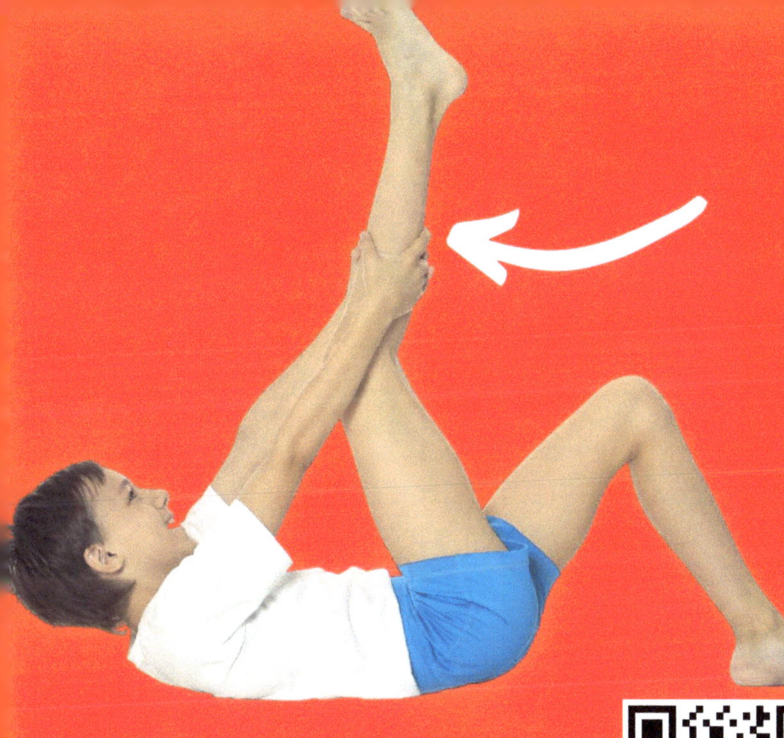

calf
Wade

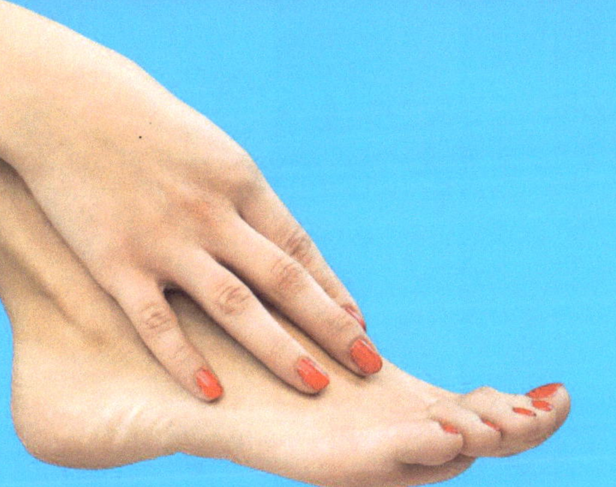

nails
Nägel

knee
Knie

necklace

Halskette

bracelet

Armband

hat

Hut

scarf

Schal

coat

Mantel

pullover

Pullover

pants

Hose

dress

Kleid

rain boots

Regenstiefel

socks

Socken

shoes

Schuhe

mittens

Handschuhe

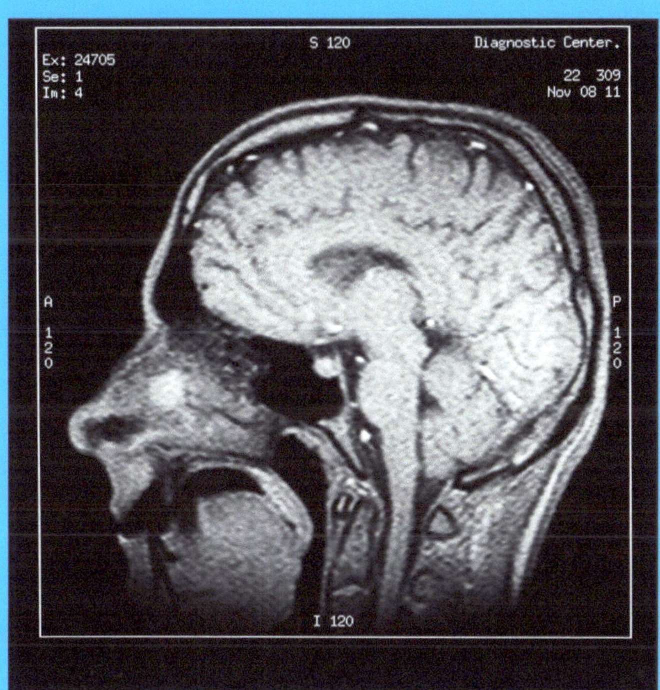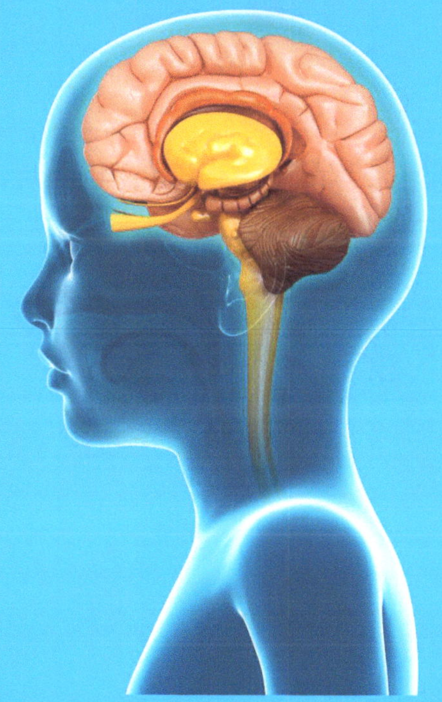

brain

Gehirn

heart

Herz

lungs

Lunge

skin

Haut

sunscreen

Sonnencreme

sun glasses

Sonnenbrille

soap
Seife

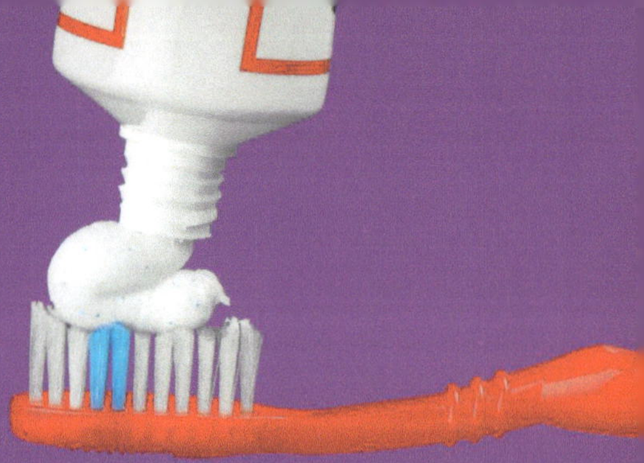

toothpaste
Zahnpasta

toothbrush
Zahnbürste

pain

Schmerz

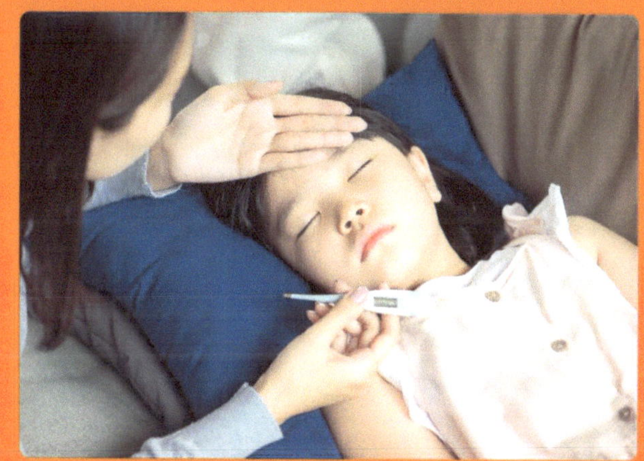

fever

Fieber

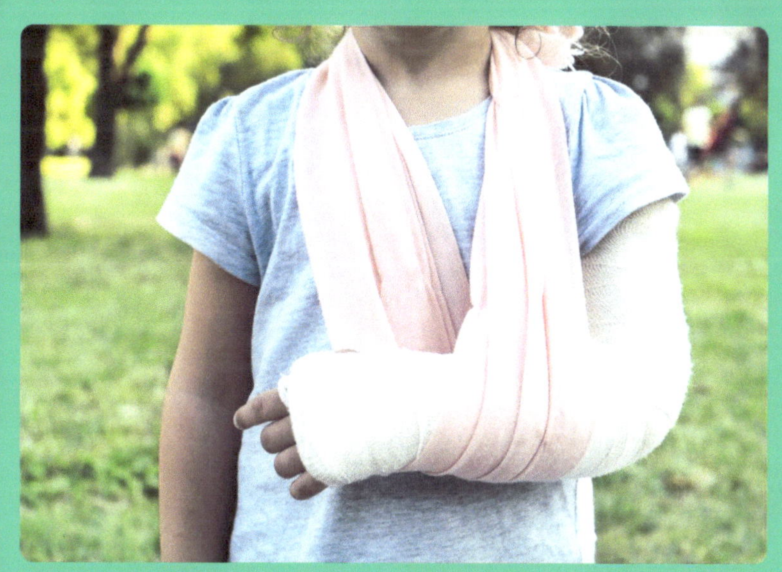

broken arm

gebrochener Arm

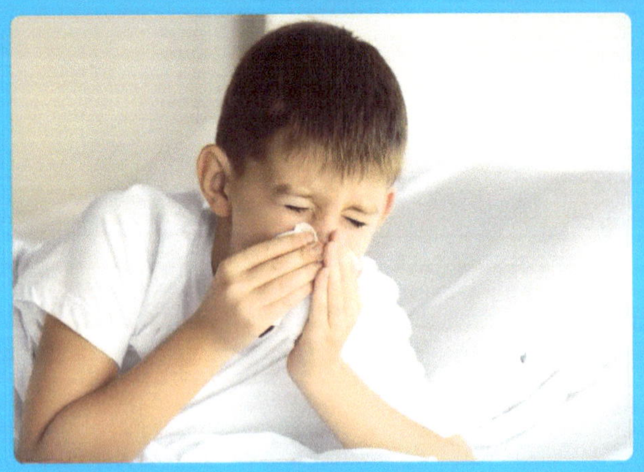

sneeze

Niesen

cough

Husten

dental cavity

Zahnhöhle

pharmacist

Apotheker

medicine

Medizin

hospital

Krankenhaus

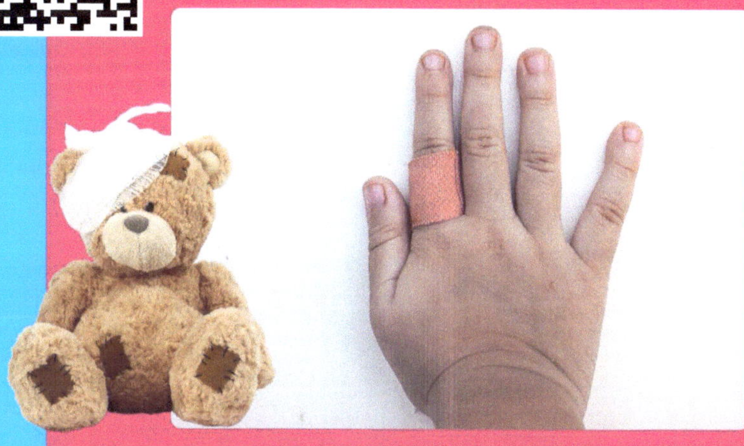

bandage

Verband

paramedic

Rettungssanitäter

firefighter

Feuerwehrmann

firetruck

Feuerwehrauto

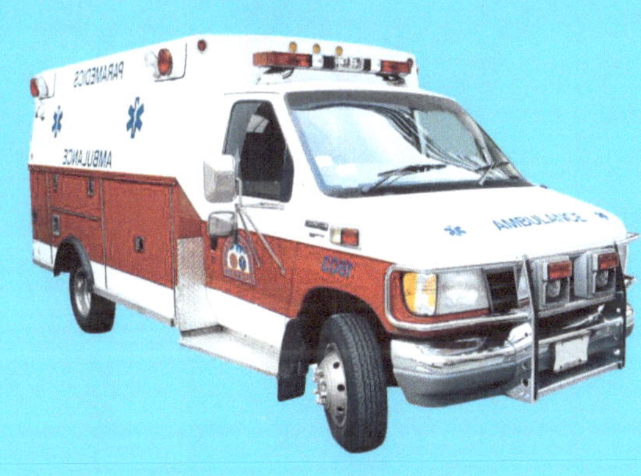

ambulance

Krankenwagen

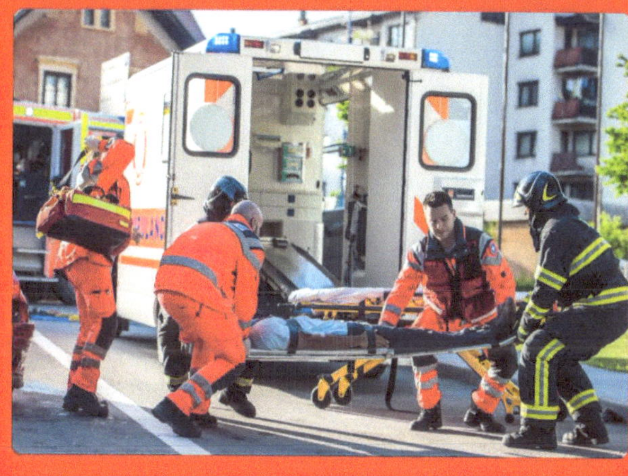

rescue team

Rettungsteam

helicopter

Hubschrauber

boat

Boot

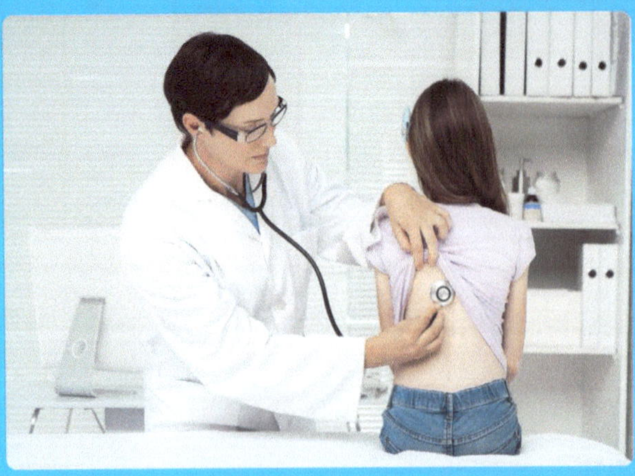

doctor

Doktor

nurse

Krankenschwester

x-ray

Röntgen

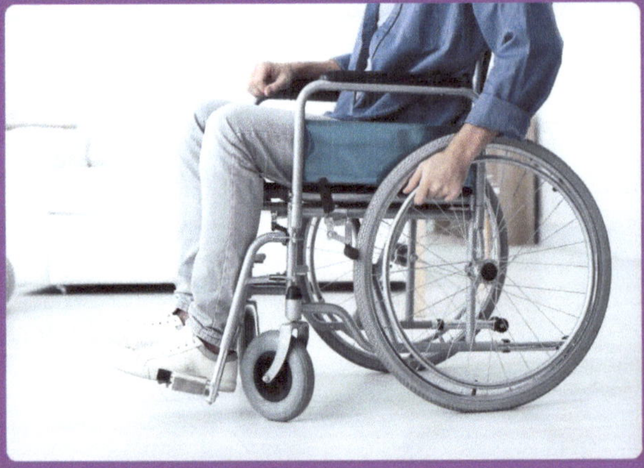

wheelchair

Rollstuhl

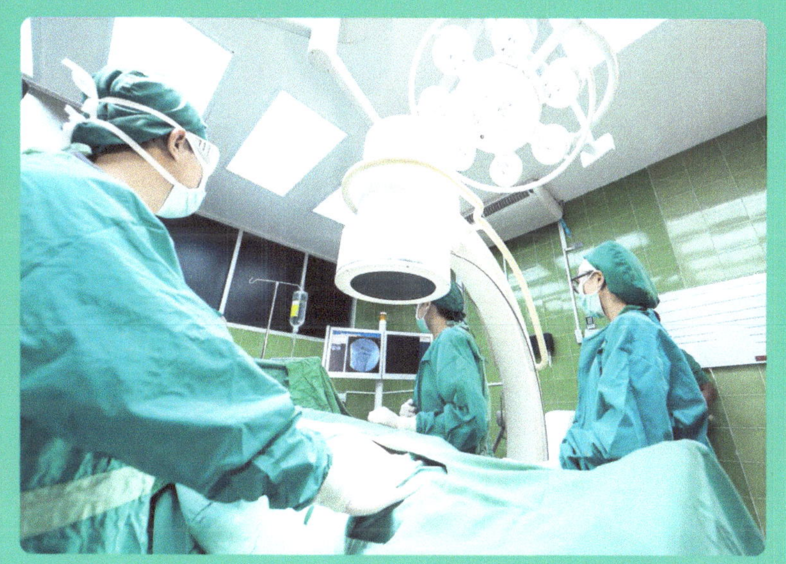

surgeon

Chirurg

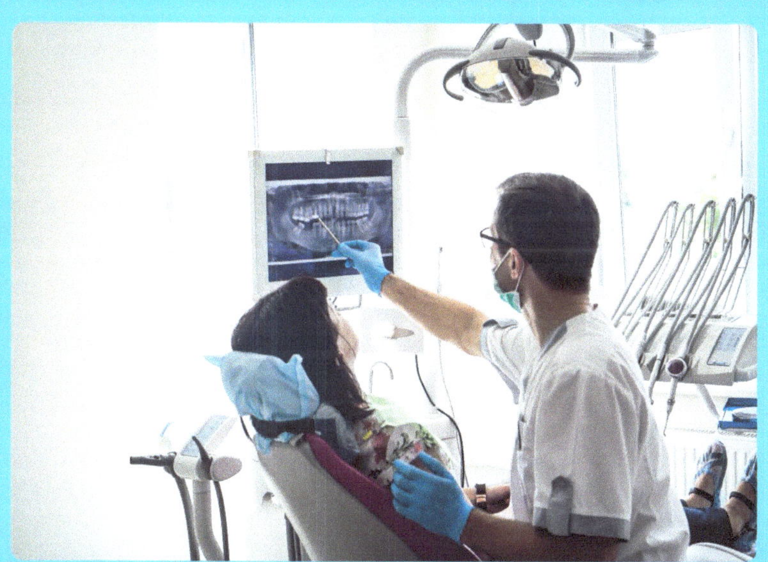

dentist

Zahnarzt

thermometer

Thermometer

scale

Waage

first aid kit

Erste-Hilfe-Kasten

vet

Tierärztin

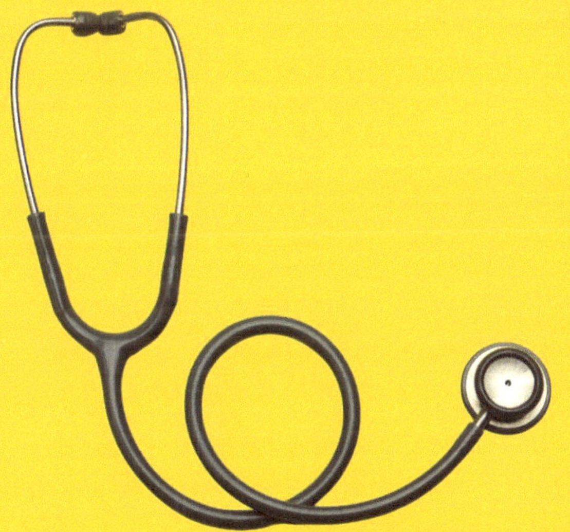

stethoscope

Stethoskop

dancing

Tanzen

basketball

Basketball

soccer

Fußball

swimming

Schwimmen

skiing

Skifahren

judo

Judo

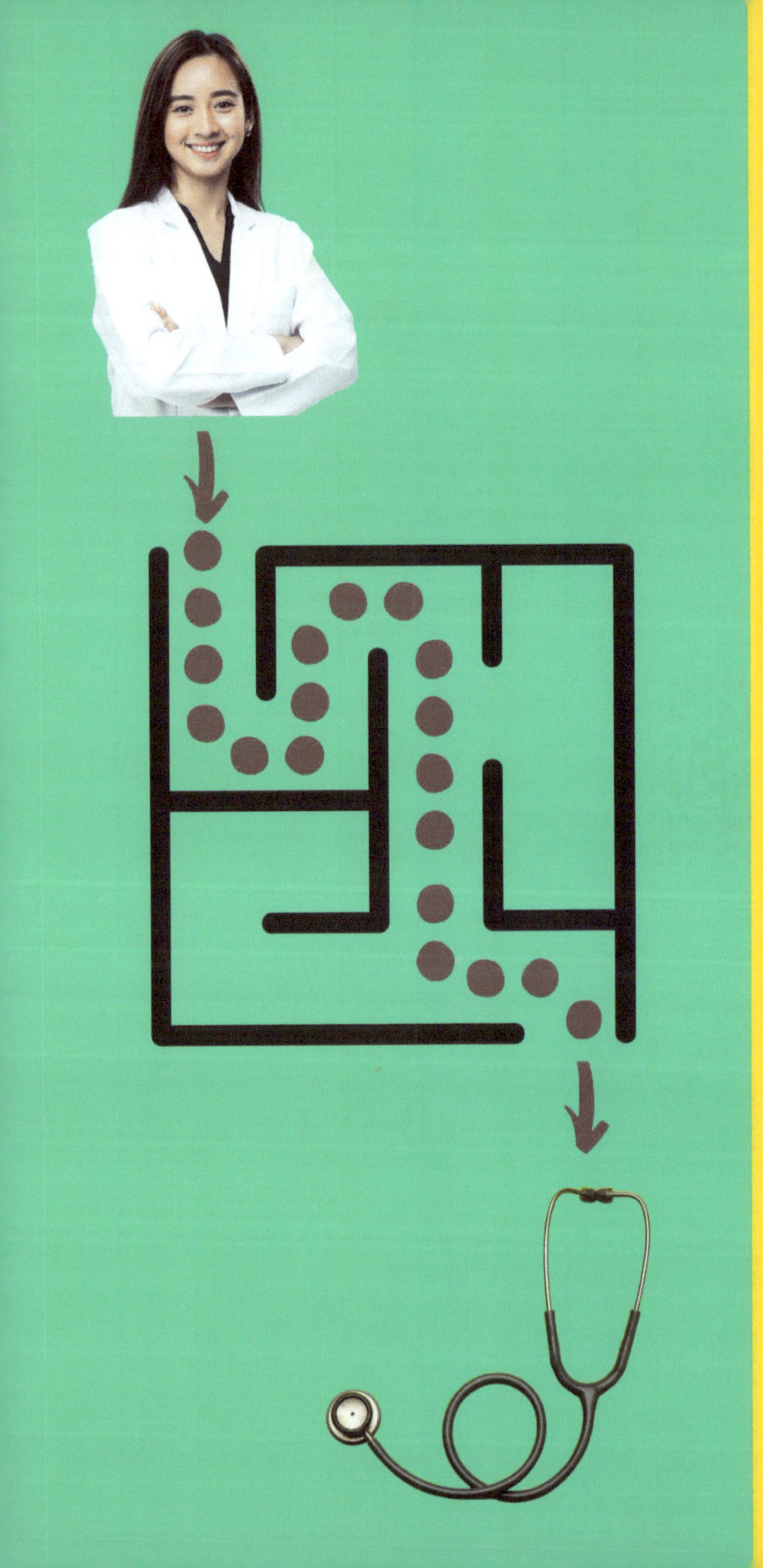

www.ingramcontent.com/pod-product-compliance
Lightning Source LLC
LaVergne TN
LVHW071631180726
843512LV00002B/285